The First
INDEPENDENCE DAY
Celebration

by Kathy Allen
illustrated by Tom Sperling

PICTURE WINDOW BOOKS
a capstone imprint

Special thanks to our advisers for their expertise:

Kevin Byrne, Ph.D., Professor of History
Gustavus Adolphus College, St. Peter, Minnesota

Terry Flaherty, Ph.D., Professor of English
Minnesota State University, Mankato

Editor: Jill Kalz
Designers: Abbey Fitzgerald and Tracy Davies
Art Director: Nathan Gassman
Production Specialist: Jane Klenk
The illustrations in this book were created with ink and watercolor.

Photo Credits: cover (leather texture), Shutterstock/Leigh Prather; 2 (parchment texture),
Shutterstock/AGA

Picture Window Books
151 Good Counsel Drive
P.O. Box 669
Mankato, MN 56002-0669
877-845-8392
www.picturewindowbooks.com

Printed in the United States of America in North Mankato, Minnesota.
092009
005618CGS10

Library of Congress Cataloging-in-Publication Data
Allen, Kathy.
The first Independence Day celebration / by Kathy Allen ; illustrated by Tom Sperling.
p. cm. — (Our American story)
Includes index.
ISBN 978-1-4048-5542-7 (library binding)
1. Fourth of July—Juvenile literature. 2. Fourth of July celebrations—Juvenile literature.
I. Sperling, Thomas, 1952– ill. II. Title.
E286.A113 2010
394.2634—dc22
2009029401

Thomas Jefferson wrote day and night. Every word had to be just right. The Declaration of Independence was special. With it, the American colonies would tell Great Britain they wanted their freedom. They wanted their own country. And they were ready to fight for it.

The Colonies belonged to Great Britain. They were ruled by King George III and the British government.

NEW YORK

MASSACHUSETTS
NEW HAMPSHIRE
RHODE ISLAND
CONNECTICUT

PENNSYLVANIA

NEW JERSEY

VIRGINIA

DELAWARE
MARYLAND

NORTH CAROLINA

SOUTH CAROLINA

GEORGIA

AMERICAN COLONIES
1775

But the Colonists believed they were being treated unfairly. They disagreed with British laws and taxes. Fighting broke out.

In the summer of 1776, Colonial leaders met in Philadelphia, Pennsylvania. They talked about breaking away from Great Britain.

The decision was not easy. A break would mean war. But it would also mean the birth of a new nation.

On July 4, the Declaration of Independence was approved. The Colonists cheered. They were ready to fight for their freedom.

John Adams had helped to write the Declaration of Independence. He said declaring independence ought to be remembered with parades, guns, and bells.

A noisy holiday was born.

But the cheering soon stopped. Through the long, cold winter and into the next year, the Colonists fought hard. At times, they believed they would lose the war. Many men died.

For most families, July 4, 1777, was just another day at war. Farmers and shopkeepers left their jobs, homes, and families. They became soldiers.

Women and children made bullets for the soldiers. They cooked meals. They took care of the sick and wounded.

It was not at all like the Fourth of July today.
There was little to celebrate.

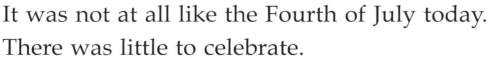

But in some places, July 4, 1777, *was* remembered as a special day. Colonists fired guns into the air. They rang bells.

At night, they lit candles in the front windows
of each house. Only the houses of those loyal
to Great Britain were dark.

In Philadelphia, 13 ships fired cannons. The ships stood for the 13 American colonies.

A short burst of fireworks lit up the sky.

In 1778, more cities joined the Fourth of July celebration.

MASSACHUSETTS

NEW HAMPSHIRE

Portsmouth

NEW YORK

MASSACHUSETTS

Boston

Providence

RHODE ISLAND

CONNECTICUT

PENNSYLVANIA

Cannon fire boomed in Providence, Rhode Island.

Ships fired their guns in Boston Harbor and in Portsmouth, New Hampshire.

Every year, more and more people celebrated the Fourth of July. They met in city squares. They rang bells all day.

They prayed for an end to the war.
Candles lit up the night.

Finally, on October 19, 1781, the fighting stopped. The Colonists had won!

The United States was a new, free country. And it already had its own holiday—the Fourth of July, or Independence Day.

Today, the Fourth of July is a day for family gatherings. People go to parks, lakes, and beaches. They watch parades. They listen to concerts. They proudly wave the U.S. flag.

At night, fireworks boom like cannon fire and light up the sky. And people throughout the United States remember the first Independence Day celebration, more than 230 years ago.

Timeline

| 1776 | The Declaration of Independence is approved on July 4. |

| 1777 | The first Independence Day celebration is held on July 4. |

| 1778 | Some cities, such as Boston, Massachusetts, and Portsmouth, New Hampshire, have large Fourth of July celebrations. |

| 1781 | Great Britain surrenders to the United States on October 19. A peace agreement is signed two years later, in 1783, ending the war. |

Glossary

Colonist—a person who lived in the 13 Colonies

colony/Colony—a land ruled by another country; one of the 13 British colonies that became the United States

Declaration of Independence—a document that says the United States is a free country and every U.S. citizen has rights that the government should protect

document—a piece of paper that contains important information

independence—freedom from another's control

loyal—being true to something or someone

Revolutionary War—(1775–1783) the American colonies' fight against Great Britain for freedom

tax—a government fee

To Learn More

∽ More Books to Read ∽

Aloian, Molly. *Independence Day.* New York: Crabtree, 2010.

Ansary, Mir Tamim. *Independence Day.* Chicago: Heinemann Library, 2006.

Heiligman, Deborah. *Celebrate Independence Day.* Washington, D.C.: National Geographic, 2007.

∽ Internet Sites ∽

FactHound offers a safe, fun way to find Internet sites related to this book. All of the sites on FactHound have been researched by our staff.

Here's all you do:

Visit *www.facthound.com*

FactHound will fetch the best sites for you!

Look for all of the books in the Our American Story series:

The Boston Tea Party

The First American Flag

The First Independence Day Celebration

Paul Revere's Ride

President George Washington

Writing the U.S. Constitution

DATE DUE

SE 27 71			
JY 13 71			
JY 31 72			
NO 2 8 72			
JY 11			
GAYLORD			PRINTED IN U.S.A.